i feel like

DANCING

i feel like

DANCING

A Year
with Jacques d'Amboise
and the National Dance Institute

by Steven Barboza
photographs by Carolyn George d'Amboise

CROWN PUBLISHERS, INC. • New York

To my family—
Timmie, who twists and shouts,
Ronnie, who sambas,
Kennie, who cha-chas,
Robert, who merengues,
Tommie, who tangos,
David, who hustles,
Craig, who tap-dances,
Diana, who boogies,
Mom, who mamboed,
and Dad, who shakes, rattles, and rolls.
—S. B.

To National Dance Institute, who puts magic in
children's lives
To my family, "the mob," and Sue and Donald, for
their constant loyalty and support
And to the late photographer Bill Weems, my
teacher and mentor
—C. d'A.

Text copyright © 1992 by Steven Barboza
Photographs copyright © 1992 by Carolyn George d'Amboise

Published by Crown Publishers, Inc., a Random House company, 225 Park
Avenue South, New York, New York 10003

CROWN is a trademark of Crown Publishers, Inc. Manufactured in the United
States of America

Library of Congress Cataloging-in-Publication Data
Barboza, Steven.
  I feel like dancing : a year with Jacques d'Amboise and the National Dance
Institute / Steven Barboza; photographs by Carolyn George d'Amboise.
    p. cm.
  Summary: Describes, in text and illustrations, the experiences of students
during the year they spend as members of Jacques d'Amboise's National
Dance Institute.
  1. National Dance Institute (U.S.)—Juvenile Literature. 2. d'Amboise,
Jacques, 1934- —Juvenile literature. [1. National Dance Institute
(U.S.) 2. d'Amboise, Jacques, 1934-. 3. Dancing.] I. d'Amboise, Carolyn
George, ill. II. Title.
GV1786.N255B37 1992
792.8'0973—dc20   91-28439

ISBN 0-517-58454-9 (trade)
      0-517-58455-7 (lib. bdg.)

10 9 8 7 6 5 4 3 2 1   First Edition

every year hundreds of children

line up for the chance to dance

for Jacques d'Amboise. Jacques is

often called the Pied Piper of Dance.

Young dancers from all sorts of

backgrounds follow him—black and white,

Asian and Spanish, rich and poor.

"Dance is magical, if taught right," Jacques says.

Jacques d'Amboise was once a world-famous dancer. Now he directs and choreographs his own very special dance company—the National Dance Institute, or NDI. All its members are children. In New York City a thousand of them at thirty schools take part. They take weekly dance classes at school and have a chance to join special weekend classes. And every one of them gets to dance in NDI's annual show, the spectacular Event of the Year.

In 1991 the Event of the Year was called *Chakra: A Celebration of India*. *Chakra* contained many surprising moments. An elephant danced nimbly. A grown man in a gold-lamé diaper pranced around stage wearing a steer's mask. A monkey king juggled crystal balls and frolicked with a hoop as big as a swimming pool. Astrologers—danced by children who in real life are partially sighted—foresaw the future. A temple danced magically. Gods descended to earth, and humans climbed toward heaven.

This is the story of what it was like to spend an entire school year preparing for *Chakra*—and discovering the magic of dance.

Jacques and his instructors select their dancers in October. Classes are limited to thirty-five, and at Public School 346 in Brooklyn, competition for those thirty-five places is as fierce as tryouts for the basketball team or the cheerleading squad. One hundred and twenty students are there for the audition.

Jacques demonstrates a few simple steps. Some students can't remember the sequence. Some dance them in reverse. One boy trips over his own feet.

"What's your name?" asks Jacques.

"Kenny," the boy replies.

"Do it over, Kenny," Jacques says.

"Do it over?"

"Yeah, do it over. But this is your last chance. Life was not done over."

Kenny repeats the steps as his classmates watch. This time he does them correctly. His classmates applaud.

Students are not invited to join NDI simply because they are fancy dancers. What matters to Jacques is a dancer's desire to sweat like a professional. If an auditioner is willing to work hard, he or she can learn the steps, no matter how difficult they are. When one student, Adrian, dances too slowly, Jacques offers him some advice.

"Go ahead," he says. "Take the atomic pill."

Adrian swallows an invisible pill and dances the steps at high speed—perfectly.

By the end of the second audition at P.S. 346, Jacques and the other NDI instructors have chosen their dancers. To those who didn't make it, Jacques says, "You are my gold team." He explains that if the other dancers don't work hard enough, the gold team will take over.

Thirty-five students remain standing on the stage. They will dance in *Chakra*.

The first steps toward *Chakra* are taken at rehearsals. Each school's dancers will perform a different routine in the Event. An NDI instructor visits each school once a week to teach the dancers their roles. Jacques teaches nine or ten classes a week, moving from school to school in order to teach at all thirty during the year.

At first the dancers are awkward. Instead of moving as a group, they twirl in different directions. Instead of dancing together, they dance like soloists. When the time comes for them to perform, the stage will be filled with hundreds of other dancers doing the same step—so the first lesson is to learn to dance together.

december

As the weeks pass, the dancers learn to move with the same steps on the same beat. They begin to work not as individuals but as a group—although they still step on one another's toes sometimes.

Jacques teaches his students that dance is hard work, but also that it's fun. In the middle of a grueling workout he cracks jokes and makes up games. *"Blah-doo-dah, mish-a-goo-shoo-doo!"* he shouts. The dancers understand him perfectly. He means, *Okay, we've got to do it again.*

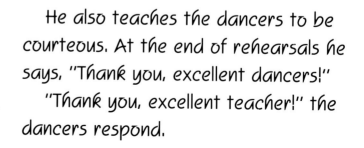

He also teaches the dancers to be courteous. At the end of rehearsals he says, "Thank you, excellent dancers!"

"Thank you, excellent teacher!" the dancers respond.

After a while the dancers find themselves rehearsing outside of dance class. They dance anytime and anywhere the feeling strikes them—at home, on the street, in school corridors.

"I like the exercise," says one dancer. "And it keeps me out of trouble."

"Dancing is almost like flying," says another. "I do it to get the energy out and express my feeling."

"I *become* the role," says a third. "I don't exactly see anything when I'm on stage. My eyes kind of glaze over. I just become what I'm doing at that time, and it's weird when you get off stage, because you have to snap back."

While the dancers are rehearsing at school, Jacques travels to India. At the Bharata Kalanjali Academy of Dance in Madras he meets a group of young dancers and their teacher. The dancers are learning a style of classical Indian dance featuring wide-open, expressive eyes and intricate hand gestures called "mudras."

Five of these dancers will travel to New York later in the year to rehearse with NDI dancers and to take part in *Chakra*. They teach Jacques the dance they are preparing, called "The Dance of the Handmaidens."

march

In New York, 7,000 miles away, NDI dancers are continuing to rehearse for *Chakra*.

The heart of NDI is the SWAT team. It is made up of the most talented dancers from the school classes. As for the name SWAT, Jacques says, "It's like the police have specialists, we have specialists."

SWAT dancers sacrifice vacations, Little League, school trips, and time they might spend at the playground. In return they get the best roles in the Event of the Year—and free dance lessons every weekend.

One hundred dancers attend class every Saturday. They wear sneakers and sweatshirts and jeans and leotards, and they rehearse for up to six hours, starting at ten o'clock in the morning. Mothers, brothers, sisters, and fathers sit along the mirrored wall of the dance studio and watch.

Jacques is demanding. He puts the class through the tough workouts of professionals.

"All morning long you've been waiting to do this dance, and when you do it, it was *mama hoo hoo!*" Jacques shouts. "That's all right because you're going to do it *better*. Try again."

They do. Jacques stops them again. "No, no, *no!*" he says. "Please make me say 'Yes, yes, *yes!*'"

"It's like a school day," says Stephanie, a dancer from Manhattan. "You actually have to pay attention. Otherwise, you get yelled at. Jacques is hard on us, but we know he's doing it for us. Sounds kind of corny, huh?"

Rehearsal time is limited, so it's not unusual to hear Jacques say, "I won't be able to get everything done, so if I start to get frantic, you know what to say."

The dancers shout, "Be sweet, Jacques!" And then they laugh.

When Jacques notices that one dancer, Shavonne, is having difficulty with a step, he asks her to dance by herself. When she finishes, Jacques smiles.

"Pretty good," he says. "But one thing was missing."

"What's that?" she asks.

"The motor."

Jacques says she didn't put enough energy into the part, and he shows her how to do it correctly.

Next time the class rehearses that part, another NDI instructor reminds them, "Reach down into your pockets and get your key."

Some dancers laugh. But they know what she means.

"Ready?" she asks.

"Yes!" they respond.

"Start your motors!"

"*Vroom-vrooooom!*" The dancers take off, stomping their feet fast and racing around like bumper cars.

While the SWAT dancers are working hard, so are the regular classes. In April Jacques goes to a school in Brooklyn for a session. This class is rehearsing the role of a desert for *Chakra*. Jacques shows John, a fourth grader, and his classmates how to move together like wind-blown sand dunes.

Chakra will be the fifteenth NDI Event. Like all of them, it will take thousands of hours of preparation. Music must be composed. Costumes must be stitched. Sets must be designed and built.

NDI has sponsored "A Celebration of India Through Masks," an art project for students who are not dancing. The students are making more than 700 papier-mâché masks, representing everything from Ganesha, a Hindu god with a man's body and the face of an elephant, to the God of Shopping, with coins for hair. During Chakra the masks will be arranged on the balcony and in the lobby of the theater to help set the mood for the Event.

Red Grooms, a well-known artist, has designed an Indian temple made out of foam rubber. It is being cut and shaped with electric carving knives. Ten knives will be broken before the temple is finished.

Other adults are working behind the scenes, too. They include David Amram, a composer. He is writing Chakra's musical score and will conduct the orchestra, which includes Indian musicians playing on drums and a stringed instrument called a sitar.

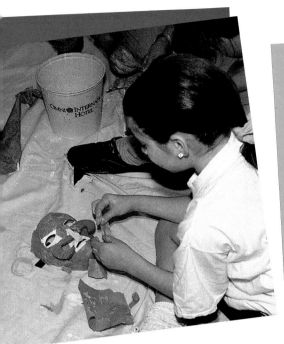
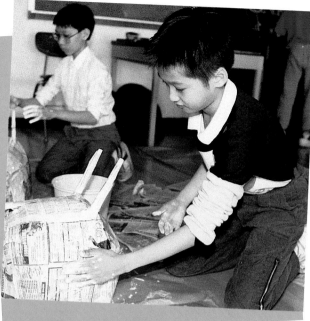

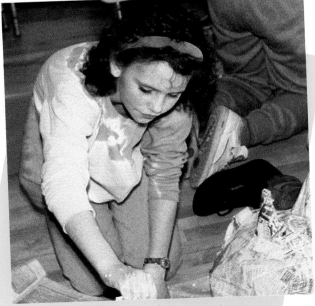

At the beginning of June the final pieces of the show are put together. Dancers who have practiced at schools all over the New York area and in the Saturday SWAT classes converge on the Brooklyn Academy of Music for dress rehearsals. They are joined by the five dancers from India, who arrived in New York a few days earlier.

On the stage 350 dancers rehearse the show's finale, nervously anticipating the performance. Jacques's voice booms through the theater. "Look up, everybody!" he shouts. "Stomp those feet. I can't see you!"

In response, 700 feet stomp and 700 arms wave. "Do I sound dramatic?" Jacques asks.

"Traumatic!" someone in the crowd jokes.

Finally, after months of preparation, the curtain rises on *Chakra*. A baby cow and its mother wander on stage, followed by a man dressed as a steer. Then *Chakra*'s narrator appears, played by Mallika Sarabhai, an actress and dancer who is famous throughout India.

"In the beginning there was the great silence," she says, "and then came the first sound."

A sound fills the theater: "*Ommm*." It sounds like a prayer.

Then Mallika adds, "And the movement became dance, and the dance made worlds move."

Barefooted, she thumps her feet, pounding out beats that sound like drumming. And one by one 350 dancers jump into the spotlights. They dance "Chaos," the dance of creation, and perform a blessing in which each cast member sticks a velvet dot—called a *bhindi*—on his or her partner's forehead.

Chakra is the story of twins, Nandin and Nandini, who undertake a dangerous journey in search of enlightenment.

First the twins emerge from an egg-shaped sack. Their dance symbolizes birth.

On their journey Nandin and Nandini confront many obstacles. They cross a mighty river, played by dancers. Then they walk over the burning sands of a desert, played by other dancers.

Afterward they must find their way through a forest, where trees come alive, animals burst into carnival dance, and a monkey king juggles to amuse himself and his kingdom. The role of the monkey king is performed by an adult, Michael Moschen.

At a crossroads Nandin and Nandini meet astrologers, danced by visually impaired NDI students from the Lighthouse school for the blind in Manhattan. Their heads poke through holes in one large robe decorated with shooting stars and crescent moons.

"Choose the middle path," the astrologers advise— and in doing so, Nandin and Nandini meet Shiva, the Hindu god of creation, destruction, and dance. Shiva is danced by Garland, a student from St. Patrick school in Jersey City, New Jersey.

Nandin and Nandini's journey ends at a temple, where the dancers from India perform their "Dance of the Handmaidens," using the hand gestures called "mudras."

The temple dances, too. It is fifteen feet high and twenty feet wide, and many cast members stand on it. They dance while holding cubes of foam that look just like the blocks beneath their feet. The temple seems to come alive.

Finally the temple splits in half, revealing a golden stairway. Nandin and Nandini climb the stairs toward a shimmering sun.

Chakra ran for three days. On each day cast members from different NDI schools danced. Altogether over a thousand dancers performed in the Event of the Year.

For each of them, preparing for *Chakra* was like going on a journey. It began with auditions. Then came months of rehearsals that were as difficult for some dancers to get through as Nandin and Nandini's journey

But when the curtain closed on *Chakra*, the audience rose to its feet and cheered. Many dancers smiled or shed tears of happiness. Their year with the National Dance Institute was over, and their year-long journey had ended in great success.

"It kind of introduced me to a whole new world," one dancer said, "and gave me the belief that I could really make it."

About
Jacques d'Amboise
and the
National Dance Institute

© 1991 MARTHA SWOPE
from *Brahms*, performed
by NYC ballet in 1977.

Jacques d'Amboise began dancing when he was seven—younger than most of the dancers he now teaches. He joined the New York City Ballet while still in his teens and danced in his first major roles at seventeen. By age twenty-one he had appeared in Broadway shows and in movies.

Jacques became one of the favorite dancers of George Balanchine, the master choreographer of the New York City Ballet. He was a principal dancer in the company for thirty-two years, until dance injuries accumulated and became too serious for him to continue.

Some years ago Jacques's eldest son was so sick that doctors thought he would die. Jacques never lost hope. Instead of becoming depressed, he visited the hospital playroom, told stories, and danced for the children, lifting their spirits. He discovered that he loved to teach.

His son recovered. Later Jacques visited his children's school and asked the principal if he could teach dance there. The principal agreed.

Many boys at the school thought dance was something for girls. Jacques changed their minds. Eighty boys attended his class, and Jacques taught them to jump higher and farther than they ever had. They rehearsed for many weeks and put on a show. That's how the National Dance Institute got its start.

That was in 1976. Since then the National Dance Institute has grown tremendously. It has a staff of four full-time instructors and several assistants, who together have led thousands of dancers to the stage. Jacques has taught young dancers all over the United States the magic of dance, and his students have performed at Shea Stadium in New York, in the Macy's Thanksgiving Day Parade, in Italy, at the Kennedy Center in Washington, D.C., in movies and on television, and at the Academy Awards ceremony.

About
the
Authors

STEVEN BARBOZA is a freelance writer who lives and works in New York City. He first wrote about the National Dance Institute in an article for *Smithsonian*. He has written many other articles for newspapers and magazines, including the *New York Times*, the *Washington Post*, *Islands* magazine, and *Essence*. He is currently working on a book about Islam in America. This is his first book for children.

CAROLYN GEORGE D'AMBOISE, dancer/photographer, has appeared in Broadway musicals and is a former member of the San Francisco Ballet and the New York City Ballet. Her photographs have appeared in numerous dance books and her travel pictures have been published in leading magazines and newspapers. She and husband Jacques d'Amboise live in New York City and have four children, George, Christopher, Charlotte, and Catherine.